MW00651903

CONTENTS

A Deceptive Doctrine or a Deceptive Booklet?

Make no mistake about it: Jehovah's Witnesses *hate* the Trinity.[1] They believe that Christians got their doctrine of the Trinity from pagans and ultimately, from the devil himself. According to the Watchtower book *Reconciliation* (1928): "Never was there a more deceptive doctrine advanced than that of the trinity. It could have originated only in one mind, and that the mind of Satan the Devil."[2]

Jehovah's Witnesses (JWs) zealously attack the Trinity for at least three reasons:

- they realize that most Catholics can't readily explain or defend the Trinity.

- they think the Trinity is easy to discredit.

- they know that discrediting the Trinity discredits the divinity of Jesus.[3]

Their chief weapon is a booklet called *Should You Believe in the Trinity?*[4] This illustrated, 32-page booklet is packed with false arguments, deliberate misquotations, and distorted Scriptures.

In spite of its many errors, the booklet's arguments are cleverly presented. This deceptive booklet could easily shake the faith of many Catholics who aren't familiar with Church history or Sacred Scripture. It might also mislead people who aren't accustomed to detecting logical fallacies.

In the next few pages, we will expose this booklet's faulty reasoning, misuse of the Church Fathers, and misinterpretation of Sacred Scripture. At the same time, we will show you how to confidently answer JWs' many objections against the Trinity.

---

[1] Jehovah's Witnesses try to pass themselves off as Christians. But they deny the most basic Christian doctrines: the Trinity, the divinity of Jesus, the eternity of hell, the immortality of the soul, and others.

[2] *Reconciliation*, (Brooklyn, NY: Watchtower Bible and Tract Society, 1928), p. 101.

[3] JWs will often ignore the primary question of whether Jesus is God in order to debate the more complicated aspects of the Trinity. Avoid this tactic, and insist on discussing the divinity of Jesus first. If you can convince them Jesus is God, honest JWs will realize they are in the wrong Church. We show how to prove the divinity of Jesus in our booklet, *Beginning Apologetics 2: How to Answer Jehovah's Witnesses and Mormons*, available from San Juan Catholic Seminars (P. O. Box 5253, Farmington, NM 87499-5253; phone: 505-327-5343, fax: 505-327-9554). We strongly recommend reading the JW section of *Beginning Apologetics 2* before reading this booklet.

[4] Brooklyn, NY: Watchtower Bible and Tract Society, 1989.

Faulty Reasoning

Error #1:
Assuming that if two beliefs are similar, one comes from the other

One common mistake in reasoning is to assume that just because two doctrines are similar, one must therefore have come from the other. For example, JWs and Moslems share certain beliefs: they each reject the Trinity, the divinity of Jesus, and an ordained priesthood. In spite of these similarities, only someone ignorant of history would assume JWs draw their beliefs from Moslems.

If two things, A and B, are similar, there could be at least four different reasons why:

Possible Reasons Why A and B Are Similar	
A ⟹ B **A caused B**	B ⟹ A **B caused A**
C ⟹ A C ⟹ B **A and B have a common cause**	X ⟹ A Y ⟹ B **A and B have separate causes; their similarity is a coincidence**

To demonstrate that one belief comes from another, it's not enough just to show similarities between the two. You have to rule out other reasons that may account for the similarities and you have to account for essential differences. JWs don't do either of these when it comes to the Trinity.

Should You Believe in the Trinity? presents an impressive—but totally false—visual argument. The booklet displays various images of pagan gods (p. 10). Some show three-headed gods, while others depict gods standing in groups of three. On the same page, they display some three-headed images made by Christians to represent the Trinity. Some of the Christian images are similar to some of the pagan images. Therefore, JWs conclude that Christians really borrowed their Trinity from pagan "trinities."

How do we respond to this claim? First we can remind JWs that the Egyptian pharaoh Akhenaten (ah KENA ten) opposed polytheism (belief in many gods), and promoted belief in only one god. He died around 1350 BC, about the time Moses was born in Egypt. Moses is responsible for the first five books of the Bible, which teach the doctrine of only one God. Does this mean our belief in one God, which JWs share with us, comes from the pagan Akhenaten? Of course not!

Although they have significant differences, Catholics and JWs both believe in some type of resurrection. We can remind them that ancient Egyptians also believed in the resurrection of the god Osiris (2400 BC). Does this mean Catholic and JW resurrection beliefs come from paganism? No. We could give many other examples.

Many beliefs that we and JWs have are similar to pagan beliefs. Moreover, pagan religions were so numerous and varied that nearly any belief of a present religion is at least superficially similar to some ancient pagan belief. But this doesn't mean that we simply borrowed our beliefs from paganism.

So how *do* we account for similarities in beliefs? Perhaps even more importantly, how do we account for essential differences?

Accounting for Similarities

Romans 2:12–16 answers this first question. St. Paul tells us that although pagans lack divine revelation, they are still able to know many things about God and His laws. They have only to examine the visible creation and the law written in their hearts (the natural moral law). Thus, they are accountable to God for their actions.

God has revealed Himself through three avenues:

- the visible world,

- the natural law, and

- divine revelation (Sacred Scripture and Sacred Tradition).

Pagans have the first two types of revelation. So it shouldn't surprise us that they would discover many basic religious truths and even anticipate, in an elementary way, many truths that can be known clearly only through divine revelation (for example, the existence of angels). It shouldn't trouble us that many pagan beliefs and worship practices are similar to ours. After all, they have the same five senses and reasoning faculties we have.

Accounting for Differences

God sent His Son to reveal the *fullness* of His revelation (Hebrews 1:1-2). Jesus entrusted this full truth to His Church (Jude 3, John 16:13, 1 Timothy 3:15). Therefore, we should expect lots of similarities between the fullness of Catholic truths and the many partial truths of ancient paganism. However, we should also expect some Catholic beliefs to be *fundamentally different* from anything found in paganism because they can only be known through divine revelation. That is precisely what we find in two central Christian beliefs: the Trinity and the Resurrection.

In spite of superficial similarities found in some carefully selected artwork, the doctrine of the Trinity is unique to Christianity. Christians believe that in the one, eternal God there are three distinct Persons who each totally and equally possess the Godhead. These three Persons are the unbegotten Father, the Son who proceeds from the Father through a mysterious eternal generation, and the Holy Spirit who proceeds from both the Father and the Son through an equally mysterious, eternal process called spiration. Paganism never taught anything that approached this Christian belief.

Then what was pagan art portraying? Various images of *three gods*—never three persons who were each completely the one God. While the art may be similar, the beliefs are worlds apart. Nothing in paganism even came close to the Christian doctrine of the Trinity. Furthermore, human reason is incapable of discovering the Trinity; if Jesus hadn't told us, we never would have known it.

The same holds true of the Resurrection. Although there were some resurrection beliefs among pagans, these have almost nothing in common with the Christian doctrine. Many Greeks, such as Plato and Aristotle, believed that the soul would go on living without the body. Other pagans believed that both body and soul would live forever in another life.

Christians believe that in addition to living eternally, the body and soul will be *supernaturally glorified* (Philippians 3:20-21, 1 Corinthians 15:42-44). This means God will radically transform our bodies and souls so we can see God face to face and know the way He knows (1 John 3:2). At best, pagans believed in *resuscitation*, being restored to natural life on earth. But Christians believe in *resurrection*, being elevated to supernatural life in heaven. This belief is unique to Christianity.

6

Error #2:
Assuming that difficult beliefs are confusing and unreasonable

JWs claim that the doctrine of the Trinity is very confusing. They also say it's contrary to reason. Thus, they conclude that it cannot come from God, because God isn't a God of confusion (1 Corinthians 14:33) nor does He do anything against reason. JWs say the Trinity is *confusing* because most people, including Catholics, find it nearly impossible to understand, let alone explain. They quote several Catholics, including John Cardinal O'Connor and Pope John Paul II, who all correctly describe the Trinity as a mystery. JWs also assert that it's *against reason* because three cannot equal one.

How do we answer these claims? We begin by pointing out the error of equating difficulties with confusion. Calling a doctrine a mystery doesn't mean it's completely unknowable; it simply means it's too deep for us to know completely. We should expect many of the truths revealed by the *infinite* God to be difficult for our *finite* minds to conceive. Some Christian beliefs, including many JWs share with us, are very difficult for non-Christians to accept. For example, both Catholics and JWs believe God made the universe out of nothing. Many people say it's absurd to think anything could be created out of absolutely nothing. JWs say it isn't absurd or confusing, but that it's true *even though it is far beyond our understanding*.

When JWs say the doctrine of the Trinity is confusing because no one understands it, we should tell them: "No one in this world understands how God could create something out of absolutely nothing, and yet you believe this without any problem. Just because something is *beyond* our reason doesn't mean it's *contrary* to reason."

What about the charge that the doctrine of the Trinity is false because it's a contradiction? Ask JWs: "If I say there are five people in one family, am I saying that five equal one?" They will answer "No," because five refers to persons and one refers to family. Therefore there is no contradiction. The same holds true for the Trinity. When we speak of three, we are speaking of *persons*. When we speak of one, we are speaking of the *Godhead*. Thus there is no contradiction.

The word "confusion" implies disorder and contradiction. A careful study of the Trinity will show it contains neither disorder nor contradiction. Like many of God's revealed truths, it *is* a difficult doctrine to grasp. Thankfully, God has given us the gift of faith so we can accept things far beyond human reason.

Error #3:
Assuming that religious truths must be explicitly taught in the Bible

JWs make an issue of the fact that the Bible doesn't *explicitly* teach the doctrine of the Trinity (p. 6). But the Bible never claims that Scripture must explicitly teach a doctrine in order for Christians to believe it.[5] Christianity has never held this. For example, the belief that Christ has both a divine and a human will and the belief that public revelation ended with the death of the last Apostle aren't expressly taught in Scripture. As Catholics, we believe that Scripture teaches our doctrines at least *implicitly*, but not necessarily explicitly.[6]

Not only are they wrong about the need for doctrines to be expressly taught in the Bible, but JWs don't even practice what they preach. Not all JW beliefs are explicitly taught in Scripture. For example, they maintain that only 144,000 people can go to heaven, and that anyone who became a JW after 1935 can only hope to live forever on earth. They also prohibit blood transfusions. The Bible doesn't teach these doctrines anywhere. Yet these beliefs are central to the JW religion.

Error #4:
Using biased sources as objective authorities

In order to support their claim that the doctrine of the Trinity comes from paganism, JWs have selected some very questionable sources. They quote Hans Küng as a "Catholic theologian," even though the Vatican removed his license to teach theology in 1980 because of his heretical views (p. 4). They quote the rabidly anti-Catholic Edward Gibbon as if he were an objective historian (p. 11). They cite other sources that reject the Christian doctrine of the Trinity. Some of these sources claim that nowhere does the New Testament teach this doctrine.

---

[5] One essential religious truth not found in the Bible is the list of the inspired books of the Bible (known as the canon). There is no such thing as an inspired table of contents. The Bible nowhere tells us which books are to be considered inspired and therefore included as Sacred Scripture. This alone disproves the idea of the Bible being the sole rule of faith. So who determined the canon of the Bible? The Catholic Church, guided by the Holy Spirit, determined the inspired books of the Bible in a series of councils and papal decisions around the year 400 AD. All Christians who accept the inspiration of the 27 books of the New Testament are really accepting, *as an infallible religious truth*, the judgment of the Catholic Church. If the judgment of the Catholic Church is infallible when it comes to the *contents* of the Bible, then Christians have no grounds for rejecting her judgment when it comes to the *interpretation* of the Bible.

[6] Explicit means fully and clearly defined or formulated. Implicit means contained in the nature of something though not immediately apparent. Jesus promised that the Holy Spirit would help the Church better understand what is implicit in the Gospel: "But the Counselor, the Holy Spirit, whom the Father will send in my name, he will teach you all things, and bring to your remembrance all that I have said to you." (John 14:26).

Later in this booklet we will show that the New Testament clearly *does* teach the Trinity.

Why don't JWs go to official Catholic documents when they pretend to give the Catholic position? Why don't they quote the early Trinitarian councils that condemned the anti-Trinitarian heretics? Why don't they refer to St. Augustine and his monumental work on the Trinity or the teachings of St. Thomas Aquinas, the great doctor of the Church? Instead they persist in citing obscure men—a motley collection of ex-theologians, anti-Catholics, and non-Christians—all of whom clearly have an axe to grind against this historic Christian doctrine. If JWs had read St. Augustine, St. Thomas, and the early Trinitarian councils, they would have learned that the Trinity is a biblical doctrine that is the heart of the Christian faith. Anyone who rejects it has departed from Christianity.

Misuse of the Early Church Fathers

JWs insist that the early Christians didn't teach the doctrine of the Trinity (pp. 6–7). They quote a theological dictionary that states the early Christians didn't have an explicit teaching on the Trinity. They also quote the *New Catholic Encyclopedia* as saying early Christianity didn't use the formulation "one God in three Persons."[7] JWs allege the early Church Fathers didn't believe in the divinity of Jesus.[8] To support this, they quote six early Church Fathers on page 7, but seriously misrepresent them.

---

[7] JWs conveniently leave out what the *New Catholic Encyclopedia* goes on to say: "If it is clear on the one side that the dogma of the Trinity in the stricter sense of the word was a late arrival, product of three centuries' reflection and debate, it is just as clear on the opposite side that confession of Father, Son, and Holy Spirit—and hence an elemental Trinitarianism—went back to the period of Christian origins" (XIV, p. 300). It is true that the earliest Fathers didn't use the word "Trinity" or the precise formula "one God in three persons" since this terminology was developed in response to later heretics. However, from the very beginning the early Church taught that the Father, Son, and Holy Spirit were each divine persons and yet that there was only one God.

JWs are masters of misquotation. They aren't afraid to cut and paste an author's words or completely twist them out of context. JWs don't care about what authors *actually* say, but only about what they can make them *appear* to say. Never accept JW quotations at face value. Always double check.

[8] It is simply false to say the early Church Fathers didn't believe in the Trinity. **Many of the pre-Nicene Fathers explicitly use the word "Trinity" to describe the Church's belief in a tri-person God.** The first use of the Greek word *trias* (translated as *trinitas* in Latin and *trinity* in English) appears in the writings of Theophilus of Antioch around 181 AD. He speaks of "the Trinity: God [the Father], His Word, and His Wisdom" (*To Autolycus*, 2, 15; William A. Jurgens, editor, *The Faith of the Early Fathers* [Collegeville, Minnesota: Liturgical Press, 1970], Volume I, p. 75, #180). The word was probably in use before Theophilus' time. Shortly afterward, the word appears in its Latin form of *trinitas* in the writings of Tertullian: "the Unity is distributed in a Trinity. Placed in order, the Three are Father, Son, and Spirit.

St. Justin Martyr

JWs claim St. Justin Martyr (100–165 AD) taught that Jesus was only an angel. They quote him as calling Jesus "other than the God who made all things." They give no reference for this quotation.

We know in his *Dialogue with Trypho the Jew*, St. Justin lists the many titles Sacred Scripture gives to the Son of God, one of which is "Angel" (along with "Son," "Wisdom," **"God,"** "Lord," and "Word").[9] When God appeared in the Old Testament, He was sometimes represented by an angel (for example, see Genesis 18:1–19:1); this is all Justin is referring to. Justin clearly believed that Jesus is God. In his *First Apology*, he writes:

> Our Teacher of these things, born for this end, is Jesus Christ, who was crucified under Pontius Pilate, the procurator in Judea in the time of Tiberius Caesar. **We will prove that we worship Him reasonably**; for we have learned that He is the Son of the True God Himself....
>
> ... the Father of all has a Son, who is both the first-born Word of God and **is God**.[10]

JWs try to prove that Justin didn't believe Jesus is God by quoting him as saying that Jesus "never did anything except what the Creator ... willed him to do and say." If quoted correctly (again they give no reference), this statement simply confirms what the Bible says: Jesus came to do the will of the Father (see John 5:19 and Luke 22:42).

They are Three however, not in condition, but in degree; not in substance, but in form, not in power, but in kind; of one substance, however, and one condition, and one power, because He is one God of whom these degrees and forms and kinds are taken into account in the name of the Father, and of the Son, and of the Holy Spirit." (*Against Praxes* [written after 213 AD], 2, 4; Jurgens, p. 154, #371). In the next century the word *trinitas* becomes very common. Origen uses it many times (see Jurgens, p. 199, #470), and his pupil, Gregory the Miracle Worker, is the first to use it in a creed composed between 260 and 270 AD: "Wherefore there is nothing either created or subservient in the Trinity, nor anything caused to be brought about, as if formerly it did not exist and was afterwards introduced. Wherefore neither was the Son ever lacking to the Father, nor the Spirit to the Son; but without variation and without change, the same Trinity forever" (*The Creed*; Jurgens, p. 251, #611). Remember, the important thing is the doctrine, not the words used to describe it. Even so, *the early Church explicitly used the word "Trinity" to describe its belief in a three-person God more than 140 years before the Councils of Nicea (325 AD) and Constantinople (381 AD) adopted it.* This proves that the JW claim—"the Trinity was unknown throughout Biblical times and for several centuries thereafter" (p. 7)—is totally false.

[9] *Dialogue with Trypho the Jew* (written about 155 AD), 61; Jurgens, p. 60, #137.

[10] *First Apology* (written between 148–155 AD), 13 and 63 [emphasis added]; Jurgens, pp. 52 and 55, #117 and 127.

St. Irenaeus

JWs claim St. Irenaeus (140–202 AD) taught that Jesus is separate from God and inferior to Him. They give no references to back up their assertion. However, we will give a quotation from St. Irenaeus that certainly shows he believed Jesus is God. And unlike JWs, we will give a clear reference:

> But not knowing Him, who, from the Virgin, is Emmanuel, they are deprived of His gift, which is life eternal. And not receiving the Word of incorruption, they remain in mortal flesh and are the debtors of death, not having received the antidote of life.... Nevertheless, what cannot be said of anyone else who ever lived, that **He is Himself in His own right God and Lord and Eternal King and Only-begotten and Incarnate Word**, proclaimed as such by all the Prophets and by the Apostles and by the Spirit Himself, may be seen by all who have attained to even a small portion of the truth. The Scriptures would not have born witness to these things concerning Him, if, like everyone else, He were a mere man.[11]

St. Clement of Alexandria

JWs assert that St. Clement of Alexandria (died around 215 AD)

> called God "the uncreated and imperishable and only true God." He said that the Son "is next to the only omnipotent Father" <u>but not equal to him</u>.

The first sentence, apparently from St. Clement's *Exhortation to the Greeks*[12] (although they give no reference), merely confirms what Trinitarians have always claimed: that there is only one God. The second sentence, calling the Son "next to the only omnipotent Father" says nothing about inequality.

The underlined phrase "<u>but not equal to him</u>" was *not* something St. Clement said. The JWs *added* this last part to make it seem like Clement is saying that the Son isn't equal to the Father. On the contrary, St. Clement affirmed both the divinity of Jesus and His equality with the Father. Consider what Clement writes in the very same work:

> And now this same Word has appeared as man. He alone is **both God and man**, and the source of all our good things. ... Despised as to appearance but **in reality adored**, the Expiator, the Savior, the Soother, the Divine Word, **He that is quite evidently true God, He that is put on a level with the Lord of the Universe because He was His Son**....[13]

---

[11] *Against Heresies* (written between 180–199 AD), 3, 19, 1–2 [emphasis added]; Jurgens, p. 93, #222.

[12] *Exhortation to the Greeks* (written before 200 AD), 6, 68, 2; Jurgens, p. 177, #403.

[13] *Exhortation to the Greeks,* 1, 7, 1 and 10, 10, 1 [emphasis added]; Jurgens, pp. 176–177, #401 and 405.

Tertullian

JWs attribute the following two passages to Tertullian (died around 240 AD):

> The Father is different from the Son (another), as he is greater; as he who begets is different from him who is begotten; he who sends, different from him who is sent.

> There was a time when the Son was not…. Before all things, God was alone.

Although Tertullian joined the Montanist heretics toward the end of his life, his earlier writings, especially on the Trinity, are considered orthodox. The first passage comes from Tertullian's work *Against Praxeas*,[14] where he responds to heretics who think the Father, Son, and Holy Spirit are the *very same person*. Tertullian rightly points out that there are three different persons in the Godhead. In this very same work, Tertullian uses the word "Trinity" to describe how the Father, Son, and Holy Spirit are three in person but one in nature:

> …the present heresy, which considers itself to have the pure truth when it supposes that one cannot believe in the one only God in any other way than by saying that the Father, Son, and Spirit are the very selfsame Person. As if One were not All even in this way, that **All are One— through unity of substance of course! …for the Unity is distributed in a Trinity. Placed in order, the Three are Father, Son, and Spirit.** They are Three, however, not in condition, but in degree; not in substance, but in form; not in power, but in kind; **of one substance, however, and one condition, and one power….**[15]

A few of Tertullian's writings show the influence of what scholars call subordinationism, which simply means that he occasionally speaks of the Son as being in some sense inferior to the Father.[16] But more often, Tertullian speaks of the Son as being equal to the Father: "So also, that which proceeds from God is God and Son of God, and both are one. Likewise, as He is Spirit from Spirit, and

---

[14] *Against Praxeas* (written after 213 AD), 9, 1; Jurgens, pp. 155–156, #376.

[15] *Against Praxeas*, 2, 1 [emphasis added]; Jurgens, p. 154, #371.

[16] The Father is the source and origin of the Godhead (see *Catechism of the Catholic Church* 2789), but this in no way indicates inequality in the Godhead. The Father is the origin (the begetter), and the Son is derived from the origin (the begotten). In the temporal world, the origin is always prior to and usually greater than what comes from the origin. For instance, a human father is always older and usually stronger (at least at first) than his son. It is easy to see why some early Fathers sometimes spoke of the Son, who is derived from the source, as being second or inferior to the Father, the origin. However, generation *in time* is very different from generation *in eternity*. The Father's begetting of the Son is an *eternal, divine process* that in no way indicates any inferiority of the Son. As the Nicene-Constantinople Creed confesses: "the only-begotten Son of God, *eternally begotten* of the Father, light from light, true God from true God, begotten not made, consubstantial with the Father" (*Catechism of the Catholic Church* 242).

God from God, He is made second by count and numerical sequence, but **not in actual condition**...."[17]

Tertullian never claimed, "there was a time when the Son was not." This remark comes from a *commentary* by a modern scholar who is summarizing one of Tertullian's statements.[18] For JWs to attribute this phrase to Tertullian himself shows very dubious (if not devious) scholarship.

What Tertullian actually wrote was that God was always God, but not always Father of the Son: "for He could not be Father before the Son was, nor Judge before there was sin."[19] Tertullian is not denying the eternity of the Second Person of the Trinity. Rather, as the context shows, he is suggesting that He received the title "Son" when the "Father" sent Him to create all things. In other words, the Second Person of the Trinity became "Son" when He was sent forth; the First Person of the Trinity became "Father" when He did the sending. But both existed from all eternity.

Some of Tertullian's terminology is ambiguous, and was avoided by later orthodox writers once controversy over the Trinity introduced a greater precision of language. We must balance Tertullian's few ambiguous remarks against his many clear expressions of the divinity and co-eternity of the Son.

The phrase "before all things, God was alone" is another one of Tertullian's ambiguous expressions.[20] Tertullian immediately goes on to clarify what he means:

...He was alone, because there was nothing external to Him but Himself. **Yet even then He was not alone**; for He had with Him that which He possessed in Himself, that is to say, His own Reason ... which the Greeks call *logos*, by which term we designate Word.... [E]ven then **before the creation of the universe God was not alone, since He had within Himself both Reason, and, inherent in Reason, His Word.**[21]

This Word was with God and *was* God from all eternity (see John 1:1). According to Tertullian, the divine, eternal Word received the title "Son" when He was sent

[17] *Apology* (written 197 AD), 21, 13 [emphasis added]; Jurgens, p. 144, #277.

[18] "Elucidations," in *The Ante-Nicene Fathers: Translations of the Writings of the Fathers down to A.D. 325*, edited by Alexander Roberts and James Donaldson, revised by A. Cleveland Coxe (original 1885, reprinted Peabody, Massachusetts: Hendrickson Publishers, 1994), Volume 3, p. 629.

[19] *Against Hermogenes* (written between 200–206 AD), 3, 3; Jurgens, p. 134, #321.

[20] Against Praxeas, 5, in The Ante-Nicene Fathers, Volume 3, p. 600.

[21] Against Praxeas, 5, in The Ante-Nicene Fathers, Volume 3, pp. 600–601.

forth by the "Father" to create all things.[22] While his terminology may be confusing, Tertullian clearly believed in the divinity and co-eternity of the second Person of the Trinity.

The key thing to remember is that Tertullian frequently uses the word Trinity to describe God. Some of his formulas were adopted word-for-word by the Council of Nicea and later councils. Tertullian certainly believed in the divinity of Christ and in the Trinity.

St. Hippolytus

JWs attribute the following unreferenced quotation to St. Hippolytus (died in 235 AD):

> "the one God, the first and only One, the Maker and Lord of all," who "had nothing co-eval [of equal age] with him... But he was One, alone by himself; who, willing it, called into being what had no being before," such as the created prehuman Jesus.

Please note carefully that the underlined words are *not part of the quotation*. JWs added this phrase to make it seem like St. Hippolytus is claiming Jesus was merely a creature and therefore not God. In this quotation from his *Refutation of All Heresies*,[23] St. Hippolytus is emphasizing the oneness of God. In no way is he denying the divinity of Christ. For in the very same work, St. Hippolytus goes on to say:

> "Therefore this sole and universal God, by reflecting, first brought forth the Word—not a word as in speech, but as a mental word, the Reason for everything. Him only did He produce from what existed: for the Father Himself was Being, from which He produced Him.... **Only His Word is from Himself, and is therefore also God**, becoming the substance of God. The world was made from nothing. Therefore it is not God.... **For Christ is the God over all**, who has arranged to wash away sin from mankind, rendering the old man new."[24]

Far from supporting the JW teaching that Jesus was merely a creature, St. Hippolytus would have condemned it as rank heresy.

---

[22] Against Praxeas, 6–8, in The Ante-Nicene Fathers, Volume 3, pp. 600–603.

[23] *Refutation of All Heresies* (written after 222 AD), 10, 32; Jurgens, p. 173, #397.

[24] *Refutation of All Heresies*, 10, 33–34 [emphasis added]; Jurgens, pp. 173–174, #398–399.

14

Origen

Like Tertullian, Origen (185–253 AD) wasn't canonized by the Church.[25] However, he is still considered a great theologian. Christians generally acknowledge that he taught correctly about the Trinity. JWs attribute two short quotations to Origin, attempting to show that he rejected the divinity of Christ and the Trinity (again, without references so we can check the accuracy of the citations):

> "the Father and Son are two substances ... two things as to their essence," and that "compared with the Father, [the Son] is a very small light."

Since they don't tell us the source of these quotations, we can't verify them. Therefore it's hard to determine the context of these extremely brief and very selective excerpts. But whatever these difficult passages mean,[26] Origin unmistakably affirmed the divinity of Jesus and the Trinity. The following extended passage from *The Fundamental Doctrines* is one of many that prove this:

> The specific points which are clearly handed down through the apostolic preaching are these: First, that there is one God who created and arranged all things, and who, when nothing existed, called all things into existence; ... and that in the final period this God, just as He had promised beforehand through the Prophets, sent the Lord Jesus Christ. ...Secondly, that Jesus Christ himself, who came, was born of the Father before all creatures; and after He had ministered to the Father in the creation of all things—for through Him were all things made—in the final period He emptied Himself and was made man. **Although He was God, He took flesh; and having been made man, He remained what He was, God**. He took a body like our body, differing only in this, that it was born of a Virgin and the Holy Spirit.

> Moreover, this Jesus Christ was truly born and truly suffered; and He endured this ordinary death, not in mere appearance, but did truly die; for He truly rose again from the dead, and after His resurrection He conversed with His disciples, and was taken up. Third, they handed it down **that the Holy Spirit is associated in honor and dignity with the Father and the Son**.

> In His [the Holy Spirit's] case, however, it is not clearly distinguished whether or not He was born or even whether He is or is not to be regarded as a Son of God; for these are points of

---

[25] Origen taught that all rational creatures are saved, including the fallen angels and unrepentant sinners. This is a heresy known as "universalism" and was first condemned by a synod at Constantinople (543 AD).

[26] Remember, pre-Nicene fathers sometimes used terms like substance, essence, and nature with different meanings, but the context always shows they are teaching orthodox Trinitarian doctrine. These words did not have precise, technical meanings until the Councils of Nicea and Constantinople defined them. Therefore, we cannot simply assume that Origen is using the words "substance" and "essence" with the precise meaning they would later acquire. We certainly shouldn't assume that he is using these words to deny the Trinity.

careful inquiry into sacred Scripture, and for prudent investigation. And it is most clearly taught in the Churches that this Spirit inspired each one of the holy men, whether Prophets or Apostles; and that there was not one Spirit in the men of old, and another in those who were inspired after the coming of Christ.[27]

This passage, written between 220–230 AD, makes the following important points:

- there is only one God.

- Jesus is a person distinct from the Father. Jesus is also God.

- the Holy Spirit is a person distinct from the Father and the Son, but associated in honor and dignity with them. Given the context of this passage, which is a discussion of the Godhead, Origen is clearly teaching the divinity of the Holy Spirit.

In the final paragraph of this passage, Origen mentions that the exact relation of the Holy Spirit to the other two Persons in the Trinity isn't fully understood and requires further study. So while Origen teaches the doctrine of the Trinity, he admits that in his time scholars still had some conclusions to work out.

At the introduction to this passage, Origen confirms that he is handing on Apostolic teachings. He indicates the one exception: the relation of the Holy Spirit to the other two Persons of the Trinity. This wasn't clearly explained by the Apostles (the Church would later clarify this relation when it had to deal with the heresies against the Holy Spirit).

Origen's passage on the Trinity is very significant for the following reasons:

- He wrote 120–130 years after the death of the last Apostle, and he is considered one of the greatest theologians of his time.

- He confirms that these teachings came from the Apostles themselves.

- This document created absolutely no controversy in an age much given to controversy. Origen presents these doctrines as something taken for granted by all Christians. He doesn't present them as something new nor does he feel the least bit compelled to defend them.

- Origin is writing 100 years before the Council of Nicea (325 AD) and 150 years before the Council of Constantinople (381 AD).

---

[27] *The Fundamental Doctrines* (written between 220–230 AD), 1 Preface, 4 [emphasis added]; Jurgens, p. 191, #445.

JWs claim the teaching of the Trinity was unknown before the supposedly pagan Emperor Constantine persuaded an unwilling Council of Nicea to accept the divinity of Jesus. JWs allege the Church didn't formulate the complete doctrine of the Trinity until the Council of Constantinople accepted the divinity of the Holy Spirit. This passage from Origen proves that the JW claim is false.[28]

Summary of the Early Church Fathers

We have shown that JWs misrepresent the early Church fathers through selective quotations and outright distortions. All six of the early Church Fathers[29] quoted by JWs to discredit the divinity of Christ in reality *affirm* the divinity of Christ. The Witnesses are contradicted by their own witnesses!

When JWs quote the early Fathers of the Church, why don't they ever give any references? Are they afraid someone will look up their quotations and discover they have completely misconstrued the Fathers?

Why don't JWs mention St. Ignatius of Antioch, a co-worker of John the Apostle and one of the earliest and best-known Fathers? Is it because his writings are chock-full of Catholic doctrines? Perhaps they are afraid of passages like: "For **our God, Jesus Christ**, was conceived by Mary in accord with God's plan."[30]

JWs fail to understand that *many early Christian doctrines were not precisely defined until they were attacked by heretics*. Only then did the Church feel compelled to state the belief in an explicit formula to rule out heresy and preserve the Apostolic teaching.

This is especially true of the Trinity. In the Bible we don't find the explicit formula "in the One God there are three distinct persons: the Father, the Son, and the Holy Spirit." But the New Testament repeatedly teaches the oneness of God.[31] It also clearly teaches the divinity of both Jesus[32] and the Holy Spirit.[33] Likewise, before Nicea, the early Church Fathers repeatedly teach that there is one God; they

---

[28] See footnote 8 for more quotations from *pre-Nicea* Church fathers who explicitly use the word "Trinity" to describe the three co-equal persons in the one Godhead.

[29] Strictly speaking, as we said before, Origen and Tertullian are not considered "fathers."

[30] *Letter to the Ephesians* (written about 110 AD), 18, 2; Jurgens, p. 18, #42 (also see #37a, #52, and #81 for other unmistakable affirmations of Christ's divinity by St. Ignatius).

[31] For example, see Mark 12:29, 1 Corinthians 8:4-6, and James 2:19.

[32] For example, see John 8:58, John 10:38, and Colossians 2:9.

[33] For example, see Acts 5:3-4, Acts 28:25-28, and 1 Corinthians 2:10-13.

repeatedly wrote that Jesus is God; they repeatedly describe the Holy Spirit in contexts that indicate His equality with the Father and the Son. Yet they felt no need to express their belief in the Trinity in a precise formula.

Then in 318 AD, a renegade priest named Arius began to deny the divinity of Jesus and the Trinity. This heresy, known as Arianism, began to spread throughout the Church. The Church's response was to express its original belief in Christ's divinity and the Trinity in a precise and explicit creed, known today as the Nicene Creed. The Church did this so orthodox Christians could distinguish the Apostolic teachings on the Trinity from heretical distortions.

Remember, what the Church expresses in creeds and formulas, *the Church lives in the liturgy* (the public worship of the Church). From the beginning, Christian worship was Trinitarian. The *Didache* (DID a kay), an ancient teaching manual most likely written during the lifetime of the Apostles, tells Christians to baptize in the name of the Father, Son and Holy Spirit, just as Jesus commanded in Matthew 28:19.[34] In *The Apostolic Tradition*, written about 215 AD, St. Hippolytus describes in great detail how the earliest Christians celebrated the liturgy. Even a casual reading of this document reveals that the early Christian liturgy was thoroughly Trinitarian. They offered prayers and administered sacraments in the name of the Father, Son, and Holy Spirit.

Finally, four of the six early Church Fathers that JWs claim rejected the Trinity are Catholic saints. The Catholic Church canonized them and gave them feast days in the Church calendar, an honor given to only a few of the hundreds of canonized saints. Would the Catholic Church have celebrated these early Fathers if they had denied one of her central doctrines? Of course not!

Misinterpretation of Sacred Scripture

Should You Believe in the Trinity? also tries to refute the doctrine of the Trinity by appealing to Sacred Scripture (pp. 12–31). JWs divide their attack into three parts. They attempt to:

(1) prove that Jesus isn't God;

(2) show that the Holy Spirit isn't a person; and

(3) discredit Bible verses Christians use to support the Trinity.

We will respond to the three parts of this section in order.

---

[34] *Didache* or *Teaching of the Twelve Apostles* (written about 50–100 AD), 7, 1; Jurgens, p. 2, #4.

The Divinity of Jesus

Our previous booklet, *Beginning Apologetics 2,* gives some of the many Old and New Testament verses—taken from the JWs' own badly translated Bible[35]—that prove the divinity of Jesus (pp. 9-12). Study this part thoroughly so you can show JWs how wrong they are when they claim Jesus is not God. Remember, proving the deity of Christ proves two-thirds of the Trinity. It shows there are at least two Persons in the one God. We can add the following observations to our remarks in *Beginning Apologetics 2.*

JWs continually refer to Bible verses that describe Jesus as subordinate to the Father (see John 14:28, Matthew 20:23). The Catholic Church teaches that Jesus is true God and true man: one divine person who possesses both a divine nature and a human nature. As *man*, Jesus is inferior to the Father; as *God*, Jesus is perfectly equal to the Father. Jesus is subordinate to the Father *in His humanity*. Jesus is equal to the Father *in His divinity* (John 1:1, 18; John 10:30; John 14:9; Colossians 2:9; Hebrews 1:6). We must read the passages describing Jesus' subordination to the Father in the light of those describing His equality with the Father.

JWs repeatedly cite Bible passages (such as Jesus praying to the Father in Luke 22:42) that show Jesus and the Father as *distinct persons*. They say this proves Jesus couldn't be God because He isn't God *the Father*. Not only is this objection ridiculous, but also it shows how poorly JWs grasp the Christian doctrine of the Trinity. Jesus obviously isn't the Father. The Catholic Church has always taught that Jesus and the Father are distinct persons! The doctrine of the Trinity claims that *three distinct persons* exist in one God. But while Father, Son, and Holy Spirit are distinct as persons, they are one in their Godhead.

JWs point to the temptations of Jesus in the desert (Matthew 4:1–11), and ask: "If Jesus is God, how could He be tempted?" Obviously, God is completely above

---

[35] *New World Translation* made by the anonymous New World Bible Translation Committee (Brooklyn, NY: Watchtower Bible and Tract Society, 1984 edition). The *New World Translation (NWT)*, which the Watchtower continues to rewrite every few years, mangles hundreds of verses to fit JW doctrines. For example, the *NWT* substitutes "torture stake" for "cross" to support the JW teaching that Jesus was nailed to an upright pole without a crossbeam. "Holy Spirit" becomes "holy spirit" or "active force" to deny the deity and personality of the Holy Spirit. Christ speaks, not of His "coming" again, but of His "presence," which JWs believe to be invisible. The *NWT* systematically eliminates any evidence for the deity of Jesus. People no longer "worship" Jesus; they do "obeisance" to Him. The *NWT* changes John 1:1 from "the Word was God" to "the Word was a god." Finally, showing complete disregard for scholarly accuracy, the *NWT* inserts the name "Jehovah" 237 times in the New Testament where it does not appear in the Greek manuscripts.

sin. So JWs conclude that because the Bible says Jesus was "tempted by the Devil" (Matthew 4:1), He must not be God. The answer to this difficulty is that the devil only tempted Jesus *externally*, not *internally*. In other words, Jesus was never in danger of giving in to the temptations Satan presented from the outside. Rather, as the context shows, He immediately rebuffed Satan. The Bible teaches that Jesus was above sin. In the JW Bible we read:

> For we have as high priest, not one who cannot sympathize with our weaknesses, but one who has been tested in all respects like ourselves, *but without sin.* (Hebrews 4:15).

> In fact, to this [course] you were called, because even Christ suffered for you, leaving you a model for you to follow his steps closely. *He committed no sin*, nor was deception found in his mouth (1 Peter 2:21–22).

Should You Believe in the Trinity? (p. 20) maintains that Jesus never claimed to be God.[36] They say the Bible never calls Jesus "almighty," a word they claim can only be applied to Jehovah God. However, their own mutilated Bible calls Jesus both God and Almighty in the same passage:

> Look! He is coming with the clouds, and every eye will see him, and those who pierced him; and all the tribes of the earth will beat themselves in grief because of him. Yes, Amen. "I am the Alpha and the Omega, says Jehovah God, the One who is and who was and who is to come, the Almighty" (Revelation 1:7–8).

JWs claim this passage refers to God the Father. However, these verses clearly describe one who is *coming* and who was *pierced*. God the Father wasn't pierced; the one "coming" and "who is to come" refers to Christ, not to the Father. Therefore, Jesus is the Almighty God.

What do JWs say about John 20:28, where Thomas calls Jesus, "My Lord and my God!" even in the JW Bible? Their explanation is very feeble: they claim Thomas was so emotional at seeing the resurrected Jesus that he just didn't know what he was saying (p. 29). We should note that the Bible doesn't give this explanation. When Peter sees the transfigured Jesus and proposes building three booths, the Bible definitely states that he didn't know what he was saying (Luke 9:33). Building three booths isn't a serious doctrinal matter. Yet, when Thomas calls what JWs consider a mere creature Lord and God—which would be a very grave doctrinal error—there is no mention that Thomas didn't know what he was saying.

---

[36] In spite of passages like John 8:19; John 8:58–59; John 10:30–33 (compare with Exodus 3:14 and Leviticus 24:10–16); John 10:38; John 12:45; and John 14:8–12.

Nor is there any mention of Jesus *correcting* Thomas. Remember, in Revelation 22:8–9, when John attempts to worship the angel, the angel immediately corrects John and tells him to worship God alone. When Thomas calls Jesus "Lord and God" in front of all the disciples, Jesus (if He were not God) would have immediately corrected him. Instead of rebuking Thomas for blasphemy, Jesus *accepts* his words. Furthermore, Jesus goes on to *praise* those who, unlike Thomas, will believe He is Lord and God without having to see and touch His resurrected body. Would Jesus, *could* Jesus, have responded this way if He were not God? Absolutely not.

It's interesting that in this long section where they repeatedly attack the Christian belief about Jesus, JWs never mention what they really believe about Jesus: that He is actually Michael the archangel![37] JWs believe that Michael the archangel left heaven and became the man Jesus. After the death of this Jesus, Michael resumed his angelic form. Thus, what we call Jesus no longer exists—he was merely the temporary manifestation of Michael the archangel. Perhaps they don't mention this bizarre doctrine because they know it can't be found in Scripture or in any Christian teaching. JWs simply made it up out of thin air.

The Holy Spirit

The next section of the JW booklet attempts to show that the Holy Spirit isn't a person. JWs claim the Holy Spirit is merely Jehovah's "active force" (p. 20). They quote two Catholic encyclopedias and a Catholic theologian as saying the Old Testament doesn't teach the Holy Spirit is a person. JWs are obviously unaware the Catholic Church does *not* claim the Old Testament clearly teaches the personhood of the Holy Spirit. The Catholic Church states that although we can interpret some Old Testament passages as allusions to the Holy Spirit, the doctrine that the Holy Spirit is a person is revealed in the New Testament. The following Bible verses from the JWs' own *New World Translation* support the personhood and divinity of the Holy Spirit:

1. **Acts 5:1–4.** When Ananias lied to the Church, Peter told him that he had lied to the Holy Spirit, and in lying to the Holy Spirit he had lied to *God*. This passage supports both the personhood and divinity of the Holy Spirit.

---

[37] "Reasonably, then, the archangel Michael is Jesus Christ…. So the evidence indicates that the Son of God was known as Michael before he came to earth and is known also by that name since his return to heaven…." So claims the JW handbook, *Reasoning from the Scriptures* (Brooklyn, NY: Watchtower Bible and Tract Society, 1989), p. 218.

2. **Acts 13:2**. The Holy Spirit *speaks* to the disciples, telling them to set apart Saul and Barnabas for the work God has planned for them. A non-personal "active force" cannot speak like a person.

3. **John 16:13**. "However, when that one arrives, the spirit of truth, he will guide you into all the truth, for he will not speak of his own impulse, but what things he hears he will speak, and he will declare to you the things coming." This verse says three important things about the Holy Spirit:

   - He speaks,
   - He hears,
   - He is referred to as "he," a personal pronoun.

4. **Romans 8:26–27**. This passage tells us that the Holy Spirit intercedes for the saints. An impersonal "active force" cannot plead on our behalf. Thus, the Holy Spirit must be a person.

JWs point to verses that speak of wisdom as a person (Luke 7:35, Proverbs 1:20). They claim the New Testament likewise personifies the Holy Spirit without teaching the personhood of the Holy Spirit. However, this argument ignores the context of the verses. The Bible never describes wisdom as literally talking to people the way the Holy Spirit does in passages like Acts 13:2.[38] The first is a *literary* device called personification, the second is a *literal* description of a person.

The Trinity

In their final section, JWs try to discredit the many verses Christians use to support the Trinity. Let's compare how JWs and Catholics interpret Matthew 28:19:

"Go therefore and make disciples of people of all the nations, baptizing them in the name of the Father and of the Son and of the holy Spirit" (Matthew 28:19, *NWT*).

JWs say that just because the Bible mentions the Father, Son, and Holy Spirit together doesn't mean they share one Godhead. They say when the Bible mentions

---

[38] Many other verses describe personal attributes of the Holy Spirit: He *teaches* the truth (John 14:16; John 16:13), He *testifies* for Christ (John 15:26), He *scrutinizes* and *knows* the mysteries of God (1 Corinthians 2:10–11), He *foretells* future events (John 16:13; Acts 21:11), He *appoints* bishops (Acts 20:28), He *distributes* gifts as He *wills* (1 Corinthians 12:11), and He can be *grieved* (Ephesians 4:30).

Peter, James, and John together, it doesn't make them one entity. JWs claim this verse doesn't support the Trinity at all.

Catholics respond: read the verse in context. This is the Great Commission. Just before ascending to heaven, Jesus charges the Apostles with a most serious and awesome task: to bring all nations into the Church. How are people to enter the Church? Through the sacrament of baptism. This sacrament, which the Bible tells us is necessary for salvation (Mark 16:16, John 3:5), is the door by which a person enters the Church of God. Thus, Matthew 28:19 tells us that people become members of the Church **and are saved** in the name of three persons: the Father, the Son, and the Holy Spirit.

It's absurd to compare the casual grouping of three people in a narrative with the solemn grouping of the above three persons in the context of bringing all men to salvation. Notice the word "name" is *singular*. It describes a very special unity. JWs admit that the Father and Son are both persons. Yet they deny that the Holy Spirit, which Scripture mentions in exactly the same context, is a person. People are saved and brought into the Church in the name of these three persons. The context forcefully indicates their unique oneness, their equality, and their distinct personhoods. This passage describes the doctrine of the Trinity to a reasonable person. By comparison, the JW interpretation is feeble and strained. They completely ignore its awesome context.

The JW Bible

JWs' greatest misuse of Scripture is their *New World Translation*. Why does it differ so greatly from all the other standard translations of our time? If JWs have the facts on their side, why don't they submit their outlandish translation of John 1:1 to accredited Bible scholars? Recall that John 1:1 is an absolute proof-text for the divinity of Jesus. It reads: "the Word was God." JWs changed it to read: "the Word was *a* god." No respected Bible scholar in the world accepts this distortion of the text. Of all the major Bible translations in our time, only the JW Bible has this mistranslation.

JWs refuse to name the translators of their Bible. They teach that Christians should reject all the scholarly translations made by accredited Bible scholars who aren't afraid to identify themselves, reveal their credentials, and submit their work for examination by other accredited Bible scholars. Instead, JWs tell us to accept a twisted, renegade translation of the Bible made by an anonymous committee. This claim would be laughable if it weren't so tragic.

Conclusion

The JW booklet *Should You Believe in the Trinity?* is a poorly reasoned and thoroughly shoddy attempt to refute the Christian doctrine of the Trinity. Its brief 32 pages contain a host of false arguments, deliberate misquotations, and misinterpreted Scriptures. JWs haven't succeeded in discrediting the Trinity; they have only managed to discredit themselves. Against the weak arguments of the JWs, Catholics should be confident that the doctrine of the Trinity will, like Christ's Apostolic Church, last forever.

Should you believe in the Trinity? Join the unanimous testimony of the Bible, the Apostles, and the Church Fathers. Join nearly two thousand years of infallible declarations by Church Councils and the Apostles' successors—the Popes and bishops—down to the present day. Join the unchanging witness of all the saints and martyrs throughout Christian history in proclaiming a resounding "**YES!**"

A Prayer to the Trinity

Father,
you sent your Word to bring us truth
and your Spirit to make us holy.
Through them we come to know the mystery of your life.
Help us to worship you, one God in three Persons,
by proclaiming and living our faith in you.
Grant this through our Lord Jesus Christ, your Son,
who lives and reigns with you and the Holy Spirit,
one God, for ever and ever. Amen. [39]

---

[39] Opening prayer of the Mass for Trinity Sunday.

Available from San Juan Catholic Seminars

BOOKLETS

♦ **BEGINNING APOLOGETICS 1:**
How to Explain and Defend the Catholic Faith

Father Frank Chacon and Jim Burnham
Gives clear biblical answers to the most common objections Catholics get about their faith. Helps you explain your faith clearly, defend it charitably, and share it confidently.
40 pages $4.95

♦ **STUDY GUIDE for Beginning Apologetics 1**

Jim Burnham and Steve Wood
Guides you through the handbook in 12 easy lessons. Provides discussion questions and extra material from the Bible, Catechism, and early Church Fathers. Perfect for individual or group study.
16 pages $3.95

♦ **BEGINNING APOLOGETICS 2:**
How to Answer Jehovah's Witnesses and Mormons

Father Frank Chacon and Jim Burnham
Targets the major beliefs of these two aggressive groups, and shows you how to refute them using Scripture, history, and common sense.
40 pages $4.95

♦ **BEGINNING APOLOGETICS 2.5**
Yes! You Should Believe in the Trinity:
How to Answer Jehovah's Witnesses

Father Frank Chacon and Jim Burnham
Refutes the Jehovah's Witnesses' attack on the Trinity and provides a clear, concise theology of the Trinity.
24 pages $3.95

♦ **BEGINNING APOLOGETICS 3:**
How to Explain and Defend the Real Presence of Christ in the Eucharist

Father Frank Chacon and Jim Burnham
Proves the Catholic doctrine of the Real Presence from the Old and New Testament, early Church fathers, and history. Gives practical ways to increase your knowledge and love of Christ in the Eucharist.
40 pages $4.95

♦ **APOLOGETICS CONCORDANCE**

Jim Burnham
Organizes over 500 verses showing the biblical basis for more than 50 Catholic doctrines—*all in two pages!* This amazing "Bible cheat sheet" helps you answer the majority of non-Catholic objections. Fold it in your Bible and never be unprepared again.
2 pages (laminated) $2.95

♦ **BEGINNING APOLOGETICS 4:**
How to Answer Atheists and New Agers

Father Frank Chacon and Jim Burnham
Traces the roots of atheism and the New Age movement. Shows you how to refute their foundational beliefs using sound philosophy and common sense.
40 pages $4.95

♦ **BEGINNING APOLOGETICS 5:**
How to Answer Tough Moral Questions

Father Frank Chacon and Jim Burnham
Answers contemporary questions about abortion contraception, euthanasia, test-tube babies, cloning, and sexual ethics, using clear moral principles and the authoritative teachings of the Church.
40 pages $4.95

AUDIO TAPES

♦ **DEFENDING THE CATHOLIC FAITH**

Jim Burnham
Teaches you how to charitably explain and defend your faith. Topics include: becoming an apologist, proving the Real Presence, using the witness of the early Church fathers, and demonstrating the incorruptibility of the Catholic Church.
Four talks on two tapes $12.00

Tapes by Father Frank Chacon	
Defending the Marian Dogmas (2 tapes)	*$12.00*
Proving the Real Presence (2 tapes)	*$12.00*
The Incorruptibility of the Catholic Church	*$6.00*
Reality of Devil Worship & Demonic Attack	*$6.00*
How to Respond to Homosexuality & Abortion	*$6.00*
The Great Gift of the Rosary	*$6.00*
The Death Penalty & Pope Pius XII and the Jews	*$6.00*